IMAGES
of America

VIEWS OF
LANSDOWNE

IMAGES
of America

VIEWS OF
LANSDOWNE

Matthew Schultz

ARCADIA
PUBLISHING

Published by Arcadia Publishing
Charleston SC, Chicago IL, Portsmouth NH, San Francisco CA

Library of Congress Catalog Card Number: 2006933263

For all general information contact Arcadia Publishing at:
Telephone 843-853-2070
Fax 843-853-0044
E-mail sales@arcadiapublishing.com
For customer service and orders:
Toll-Free 1-888-313-2665

Visit us on the Internet at www.arcadiapublishing.com

To Judie and Helen
for all they have given me.

Contents

About the Photographs   6

Introduction   7

1.   Along the Darby Creek   9

2.   Transportation   17

3.   Lansdowne and Baltimore Avenues   25

4.   School Days   61

5.   The War Effort   69

6.   Houses of Worship   73

7.   Civic Groups and Leisure Time   81

8.   Neighborhoods and Homes   97

Acknowledgments   128

About the Photographs

A large number of photographs in this book come from the work of three Lansdowne residents. At the turn of the century, Stephen Pancoast Levis, who made his home on North Maple Avenue, was co-publisher of the *Lansdowne News* and a professional photographer. He captured many of the borough's celebrations, residences, businesses, and people on glass-plate negatives. Many of the photographs were commissioned by real estate agents or builders who used them to entice city dwellers to move to the new suburb. Other homes were recorded at the request of proud homeowners or businessmen.

George Walton, who resided on Shadeland Avenue, was a mechanical engineer and according to family lore, almost lost his job because he wanted to spend more time pursuing his photographic hobby than working. Walton captured the leisure time of his family, portraits of his children, natural settings, industrial buildings along the Darby Creek, and buildings on his working farm which now comprise the 1960s housing development on Berkeley, Eldon, and Shadeland Avenues and on Kerr and Walton Places.

A decade later, Daniel DeVaux opened his photography business in Lansdowne and recorded the borough as it went through its greatest period of change, moving from a streetcar suburb into an automobile-centered community. DeVaux was a prolific photographer of Lansdowne's homes, businesses, social scene, residents, and institutions.

Introduction

During the first half of the nineteenth century, what is now the Borough of Lansdowne was a sparsely populated crossroad at Darby Haverford Road (now Lansdowne Avenue) and Baltimore Pike, in the largely agricultural Upper Darby Township, 6 miles from Philadelphia's City Hall. In 1855, the Wilmington and Baltimore Railroad stretched a single track through what is now Lansdowne. However, because of the limitations of a single track and since railroads focused their efforts on developing freight lines, the borough would not grow until after a second track was laid.

In the 1880s the Pennsylvania Railroad bought the line and constructed a second track. The railroad company also began to promote the construction of homes in Lansdowne. From the railroad's perspective it made good business sense because construction materials had to be shipped via the railroad into the borough, and once the houses were built, residents would have to use the railroad's commuter trains to get in and out of Philadelphia. The frequency of trains passing through the borough increased, making Lansdowne attractive to real estate investors. Lansdowne quickly became the premier community for middle-class families in eastern Delaware County.

By the early 1890s, a rift developed between the real estate speculators and developers in present-day Lansdowne, and the farmers of Upper Darby Township. The real estate interests were concerned with paving streets and bringing utilities to the rapidly growing commuter village. The majority of Upper Darby Township was comprised of farmers who had little interest in the area being developed. For these improvements to be realized, taxes had to be raised, which offered little benefit to the farmers. It was decided by leaders of the business community that the village would have to separate from Upper Darby. In June of 1893, the Commonwealth of Pennsylvania granted the request of petitioners, and the Borough of Lansdowne was incorporated.

For more than a century before its incorporation the area which now encompasses the Borough of Lansdowne was the home of various industrial businesses. Along the Darby Creek, textile, paper, cotton, and dye mills thrived. Along the railroad line, silk, tin work, roofing, piping, and steel mills prospered. Lansdowne also was known as a center for the florist trade. The Pennock family, William Leonard, and August Valentine Doemling all successfully operated businesses in the borough. In the 1890s small hostelries such as The Evergreen Lodge, Hartel's Guest House, and The Windermere hosted people passing through town or those who sought refuge from the heat of the city. If you were building a home you didn't have to go far to find construction materials with Bartram's, Mitchell's, and Hoopes' lumberyards nearby. Dix Masonry, Edgar Bishop the general contractor, Pharoah the plumber, or Nacey's roofing could take care of your contracting needs. Renowned Philadelphia architects designed Lansdowne's gracious homes and businesses. Frank Furness, the greatest Philadelphia architect of his time, designed the Barker Building, the Pennsylvania Railroad's Lansdowne station, and countless private residences throughout the borough. Led by men like William Boyd, Frederick

Underhill, and Father Markee, religious houses of numerous denominations were constructed; many on land donated by residents, which created a social network and left us the legacy of a rich collection of architecture, art, and folklore.

By the turn of the century, a trolley line linking the communities along Baltimore Pike between Media and Philadelphia was constructed. In 1902, Lansdowne residents petitioned the Pennsylvania Railroad to construct a new, modern railroad station in the borough. Quickly, Lansdowne was becoming the center of transportation for eastern Delaware County. As a result, the number of houses built in the borough increased dramatically between 1900 and 1910. Lansdowne also dramatically benefited from the peace dividends following both World Wars I and II. Urban flight after World War II added to the demand for housing in the borough which had already been dubbed a "Superb Suburb."

Lansdowne's strength over many years of change, both in and out of the borough, was its residents' commitment to organizations which sought to serve and enrich the community. In its earliest days, the Neighbors Club, the Twentieth Century Club, the Lansdowne Natural Science Club, Daughters of the American Revolution, the Union Athletic Association, the Lansdowne Fire Company, and countless civic associations were created to enhance, enrich, and protect the lives of area residents. Many of these organizations remain stronger than ever and have been joined by the others such as Lansdowne Cultural Alliance, Lansdowne Allied Youth, Boys and Girls Clubs, the Lansdowne Symphony, and the Greater Lansdowne Civic Association. Leading these organizations is never an easy task, but there have been people over the years who have thrived on organizing civic betterment projects, led fund-raising campaigns, served as unwavering boosters of Lansdowne, and whose opinion was accepted by all. James Stewart was such a man. In addition to serving as burgess for many years, he served as president of the Lansdowne Fire Company and the Union Athletic Association, as the manager for numerous baseball teams, was a member of the Local Chapter of the Masons, served on the Lansdowne School Board, and was a trustee of the Lansdowne Public Library. He led the campaign to purchase land on East Essex Avenue to create a playground for the borough's children. Later, a portion of the playground was used to build the Lansdowne High School. He was affectionately referred to as "Uncle Jim," and the playground was later named Stewart Field in his honor. Professionally, he was the owner of the Caledonia Mills, a textile business in Clifton Heights. As a testament of his commitment to our borough, he appears more frequently in this book than any other Lansdowne resident.

One

Along the
Darby Creek

For over three hundred years, the Darby Creek has served as a mode of transportation and as a power source for mills. Its banks have accommodated transient animal trappers, housed industrial workers, and even been used as a backdrop in movies. It is also a place of great beauty which continues to serve as a place for recreation. This view of the Darby Creek and the bridge crossing at Baltimore Avenue was recorded c. 1900.

Charles Kelly's mansion sits high on a hill above his worker tenements and the Kellyville Mill which he operated c. 1862. The mansion later became known as Gladstone Hall and sat in present-day Gladstone Manor. The Kellyville Mill was located on the west side of the Darby Creek on Baltimore Avenue.

The Kellyville Mill burned to the ground, as recorded in this August 24, 1888 photograph.

In 1950, *The Philadelphia Bulletin* reported that tenement housing on Burmont Road was about to be demolished. The open field on the left was developed as the Lansdowne Swim Club.

Transient animal trappers built simple cabins which sat in the general location of what is today the Hoffman Park parking lot. This photograph was taken *c.* 1900, a few years before the cabin was razed.

This mill worker house, photographed in 1912, still sits at the back of the Hoffman Park parking lot.

The Darby Creek has long captured the imagination of Lansdowne's children, as evidenced in this c. 1900 photograph.

Modern bridges, such as the Hilldale Road Bridge across the Darby, encouraged the development of land along both sides of the creek. This postcard view was recorded during the 1910s.

Just after the turn of the century, W.P. Conard built this house on the Knoll, a private enclave originally created by several childhood friends.

At the bottom of Lansdowne Court this walkway, photographed in the 1910s, led to a rope bridge which traversed the Darby Creek.

The rope bridge is evident behind the children playing on the frozen Darby Creek in the 1910s. The bridge led to Pennock's Woods.

The Conard family enjoys a picnic at Pennock's Woods just after the turn of the century.

The recreation opportunities of the Darby Creek quickly became a reason for families to move to the growing borough. In this photograph, the Titus family enjoys an outing on the creek's bank.

Samuel Lubin, a pioneer movie maker, used the Darby Creek as a backdrop for some of his productions. During his filming he created quite a stir among the locals, who were hired as extras or provided other needed services during filming, c. 1910.

This covered bridge was located where Providence Road crossed the Darby Creek. To capture the allure of Lansdowne's growing popularity, area neighborhoods adjacent to the borough were identified as being part of the borough, as in this 1910s postcard.

Two

Transportation

Lansdowne's development has always been tied to advances in transportation technology. The railroad made it possible for area farmers and manufacturers to get their products to market as early as 1855, when a single track was laid through what is presently Lansdowne. In the 1880s, a second track was laid, and the race was off; land speculators began to buy land and promote the area as a commuter village. In 1902 the Pennsylvania Railroad replaced the borough's first station with the station pictured here, which was better able to accommodate the borough's growing population. Other advances in transportation would have equal impact over the borough's next hundred years.

In this rare *c.* 1902 photograph, the first railroad station, originally known as the Darby Road Station (built in 1867), sits next to its replacement. It was on this building that Richard Griffith, with the permission of local resident and president of the Pennsylvania Railroad Thomas Scott, nailed up the sign where the name Lansdowne appeared for the first time. The building sat between the Frank Furness-designed station of 1902 and the Lansdowne Avenue bridge over the railroad tracks. It replaced an earlier 1855 building which sat on the west side of the bridge, which later served as a freight station.

18

The 1867 station also served as a post office and had living accommodations for the station master. This photograph shows the building from the track side.

A steam locomotive pulls into the Lansdowne station, just after the turn of the century.

The modern station, shown here in 1952, was struck by fire in 1992. Hundreds of residents rallied and successfully lobbied the Southeastern Pennsylvania Transportation Authority to restore the station. The 1855 station, which later served as a freight station, is at the center of the photograph beyond the Lansdowne Avenue bridge.

This is the end of the afternoon commute for a group of Lansdowne residents, c. 1902. In the background is the Pennock Building. The slight hump in the road is the Lansdowne Avenue bridge, which was later raised to allow larger railroad engines to pass under it.

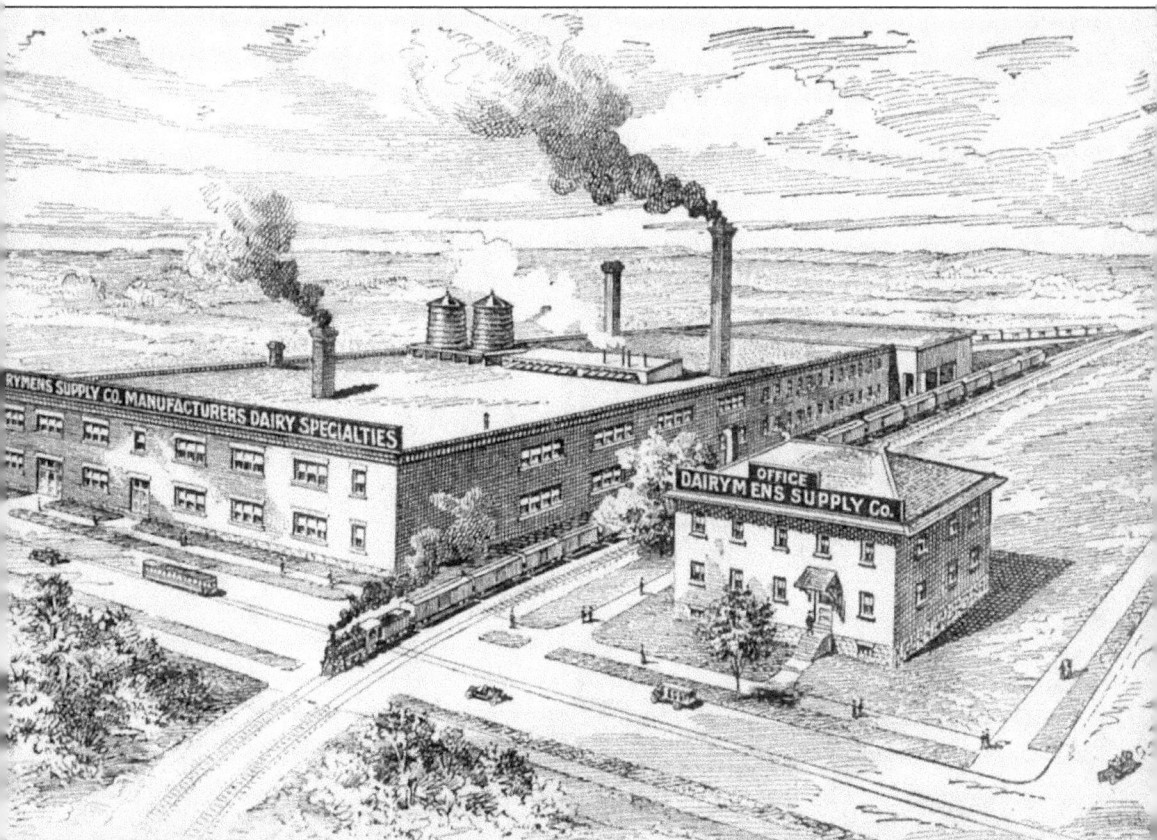

In the late 1870s, a railroad spur called the Newtown Square and Cardington Branch was laid, beginning 200 yards south of the Fernwood railroad station off of the Media-West Chester line. Originally it was to carry passengers and freight, but because of low usage by passengers, it became solely a freight line in 1902. The spur is shown as it passes by the Dairymens' Supply Company at Baltimore Avenue, now the site of the Super Fresh supermarket. A trolley car passes in front of the Dairymens' supply in this 1910s etching.

Many Lansdowne residents were very unhappy with the idea of trolleys passing through the borough. Many had fled the city because of crime and unhealthy conditions, including the danger and noise of trolleys. A line running on Baltimore Avenue was about all some residents could tolerate. In 1909 a bidding battle occurred, pitting competing trolley companies against each other. The companies offered considerable sums of money to the borough in addition to promising to upgrade streets as trolley tracks were laid. Claims of bribes to borough officials were made by competing interests. In the end, the residents won. The only trolley to pass through the borough was the existing trolley on Baltimore Avenue. The trolley shown here in 1940 ran on Wycombe Avenue from Darby to Fairview Avenue, thus never making it into the borough.

The trolley is traveling on Baltimore Avenue, passing through the borough between Windermere and Ardmore Avenues, c. 1902.

The advent of the autotruck mobilized entrepreneurs to offer new services, as shown in this 1905 photograph, taken along the Darby Creek, of the Lansdowne Borough Laundry truck.

Saturday Morning on Lansdowne Avenue, Lansdowne, Pa.

This *c.* 1913 postcard, entitled "Saturday Morning on Lansdowne Avenue," was photographed from south of Baltimore Avenue looking north. It records the era when automobiles and horses were on the street at the same time. The affordability and proliferation of automobiles changed everything. The design of Lansdowne's newer neighborhoods now had to accommodate cars. Established neighborhoods had driveways carved in lawns, and older buildings were demolished to make room for parking lots. Accessibility to the city became even easier; and the borough's population began to grow. Area farmers sold off their land holdings to real estate developers, and the borough's boundaries began to blur.

Three

Lansdowne and Baltimore Avenues

For over a hundred years, Baltimore and Lansdowne Avenues have been the center of the borough and its main business district. These two well-traveled streets have been the site of many of the borough's most significant parades, events, and works of architecture. This chapter is set up like a walking tour, beginning where the streets cross and then going north on Lansdowne Avenue from Baltimore; south on Lansdowne from Baltimore; east on Baltimore from Lansdowne; and finally, west on Baltimore from Lansdowne. We begin with an image from the streets' intersection as recorded in *The Philadelphia Bulletin* in 1951, looking southwest from the roof of Hartels on the northeast corner.

Hinkson's store, as shown in this 1898 photograph, was originally built on the southeast corner of Lansdowne and Baltimore. In 1899 it moved to about where Borough Hall's parking lot is today.

Edwin Lewis, architect and local real estate agent, stands at the southeast corner of Lansdowne and Baltimore in front of Davis' Drugstore in 1905.

Harry M. Davis poses in his store, Davis' Drugstore, *c.* 1905.

The same corner is shown here around forty years later. The store signs have been made larger so that they would be noticed by people in cars.

The 1835 Levis House was located in 1899 on the southwest corner of Lansdowne and Baltimore Avenues. The house was used over the years as a residence, doctor's office, and retail store.

The Lansdowne Bank & Trust Company razed the Levis House in the mid-1920s and opened this building on October 23, 1926. A large warehouse building was moved from just south of the Levis House to West Baltimore Avenue to accommodate the new structure, c. 1950.

The Barker Building was constructed on the northwest corner of Lansdowne and Baltimore Avenues. R.K. Ingram, who built the structure, looks proudly out of a second-story window, c. 1900.

The Barker Building was partially replaced in the 1930s by a new building, shown here in a photograph taken in 1952.

John Hartel stands in the doorway of his store on the northeast corner of Lansdowne and Baltimore Avenues in 1900.

Hartel had renovated his building and added the stores to the east by the time of this 1928 photograph.

A 1930s postcard shows how important car parking had become to Lansdowne's business district. This view from north Lansdowne Avenue shows the northern end of the Barker Building.

A firemens' parade makes its way north on Lansdowne Avenue on May 4, 1942. The rear of Hartel's building reveals a small sign welcoming tourists.

A carriage makes its way north on Lansdowne Avenue from above East LaCrosse Avenue in 1905.

Ruth Davis Hopkins Flannery, a lifelong Lansdowne resident, goes for a stroller ride on North Lansdowne Avenue in 1905. The tower in the rear of the photograph is the Lansdowne Methodist Church.

Blanchepierre, constructed in 1891 and shown here in 1897, was the home of Francis G. Taylor, an attorney. The house was razed in the 1920s to make way for the construction of the Lansdowne Theater.

The Lansdowne Theater, a Moorish-styled movie theater, opened on June 7, 1927, to an invitation-only audience. Unfortunately, the theater is currently dark, awaiting a rebirth.

As the business district and number of cars grew, houses along Lansdowne Avenue became less hospitable. As a result, many older homes were razed to make way for commercial development. This home came down for the construction of the F.W. Woolworth Store in 1927.

The Greystone, photographed here in 1911, was originally a private residence which became a restaurant and boarding house. It was later demolished to make room for commercial development. The Greystone was located between Baltimore and LaCrosse Avenues on the east side of the street.

As depicted in this 1927 photograph, North Lansdowne Avenue quickly changed from a residential district to a commercial district.

Lansdowne Avenue at Stratford Avenue in 1927 is shown just before it became a business district. Today, the building with the "For Sale" sign in front of it stands behind a gas station, and the far corner is now a WAWA convenience store.

At the turn of the century, the borough government had the dirt roads in Lansdowne sprinkled with water to minimize blowing dust. The truck shown here was known as "the sprinkle truck." The building in the rear is the Lansdowne Methodist Church.

The plot of land on which this house sits at 127 North Lansdowne Avenue was carved from the large estate of Henry Albertson. As would happen for decades throughout the borough, larger pieces of land were subdivided to accommodate the growing number of people moving to Lansdowne.

This Tudor Revival-style house at 161 North Lansdowne Avenue was constructed just to the south of the Scarborough farm. The farm included a small pond located about where the Lansdowne High School tennis courts are today.

Lansdowne Avenue, just south of Essex Avenue, served as the race course for a soapbox derby in 1902. Homes under construction on the east side of the street served as bleachers for cheering fans.

The Essex House, photographed c. 1900, was originally a private single residence that was converted into apartments in the 1920s.

Arlington Cemetery was opened in 1895 to serve as the final resting place for Lansdowne's residents. This 1910 postcard was issued as part of the cemetery's marketing efforts.

The first block of South Lansdowne Avenue on the west side of the street was decked out for the 1914 Delaware County Firemens' Association's annual convention.

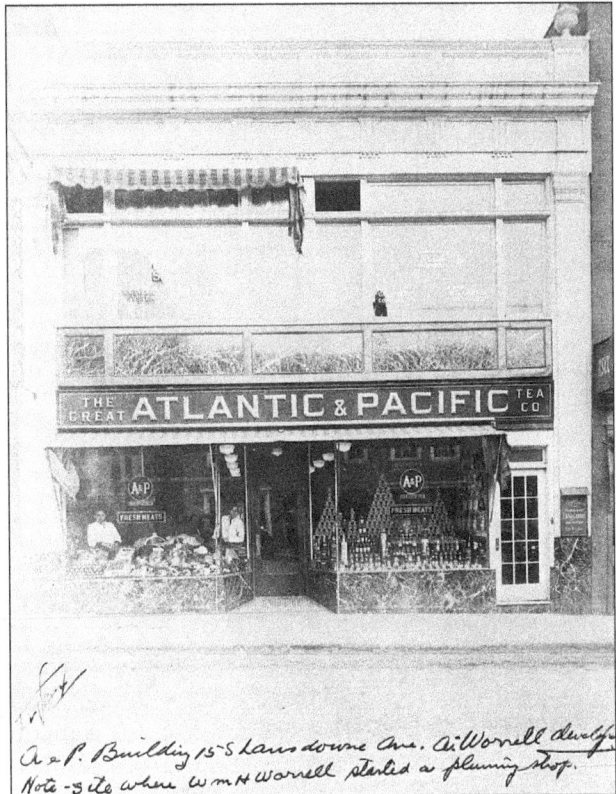

By the 1920s, national chain stores began to appear in small towns across America. An Atlantic and Pacific store (A&P), located at 11 South Lansdowne Avenue, is the subject of this late-1920s photograph.

This 1905 photograph of South Lansdowne Avenue from just north of the railroad bridge shows a trolley, an early automobile, and a horse-drawn carriage passing by on Baltimore Avenue.

In 1910, the interior of the grocery store at the corner of Lansdowne and Madison Avenues showed the growing influence of popular brand foods such as Kellogg's Cornflakes™, Heinz Ketchup™, and Chase and Sanborn Coffee™.

Caspar Pennock constructed the Pennock Building at South Lansdowne and Madison Avenues. The National Bank of Lansdowne operated from this building and installed the clock along the street. Today the building is operated by the local Masonic Lodge, which maintains the clock.

This 1903 photograph shows the Lansdowne and Darby Saving Fund and Trust Company, located on Lansdowne Avenue just north of the railroad bridge. The lawn to the right of the building was the entrance to Lansdowne Villa, a rooming house.

Garrett Hall, located at Lansdowne Avenue and Scottdale Road, had served as a space for community meetings and private business for many years before being razed in 1931. The congregation of the Lansdowne Methodist Church first met in this building in 1891 to organize the church.

In 1931, the U.S. Postal Service constructed this post office building at Lansdowne Avenue and Scottdale Road. This building served as the post office until 1956.

As you move further south on Lansdowne Avenue, the neighborhood once again becomes residential. It is believed that this large home, photographed in 1905, was designed by renowned architect Frank Furness. Today it sits just south of the Twentieth Century Club.

The Devonshire was also designed by Frank Furness. It was designed for Thomas Scott, who was president of the Pennsylvania Railroad in the 1870s. Prior to the development of Lansdowne Court, this property's front lawn extended to Lansdowne Avenue as shown in this 1910s postcard. That lawn now has several homes on it.

Athdara at 85 South Lansdowne Avenue, shown just after its completion in 1902, was the home of Seymour Eaton. Eaton was the author of the popular series of children's books, The Roosevelt Bears, and was a professor at the Drexel Institute (now Drexel University). He was also a journalist for the *New York Times* and the *Chicago Record*. After his death in 1916, his wife had the apartment buildings constructed on either side of Athdara in order to maintain her income.

Around 1908, the Scott Estate was subdivided by William Shuster and Ellwood and J. Henry Bartram, and Lansdowne Court was developed. Its setting along the Darby Creek and its proximity to the railroad station made it a very desirable address.

Lansdowne and Fairview Avenues, shown in 1905, was a popular address. It was far enough from the noise of the borough's business district but yet convenient to the downtown area as well as the Lansdowne Country Club, which was located on the site of today's Fitzgerald Mercy Hospital.

The sprawling estate at 408 South Lansdowne Avenue, as shown in 1906, had a beautiful vantage point at the top of the Darby Valley. Looking from the rear of the house, one could see the Darby Creek and the old covered bridge on Providence Road. This unique vantage point made it seem as if you were looking out from among the canopies of the trees along the creek. The house was demolished in 1989, and the site awaits redevelopment.

Having outgrown its rented space in the Barker Building, the Borough Council constructed Borough Hall at 12 East Baltimore Avenue in 1902. Borough Hall was the home of the Lansdowne Fire Company from 1902 until 1986. The building underwent extensive renovation in 1989.

Hinkson's Store, photographed during the 1914 Firemens' Convention (as mentioned on p. 26), originally sat on the southeast corner of Lansdowne and Baltimore Avenues. Moved in 1899, it was razed to create a parking lot for Borough Hall and a temporary shelter for the Lansdowne Fire Company.

Lansdowne School was constructed in the 1880s, prior to the incorporation of the borough by the Upper Darby School District on Baltimore Avenue at Highland Avenue. This 1904 photograph is taken from approximately where the Greater Delaware Valley Bank now sits.

47

The Lansdowne Public Library, then operated by the Lansdowne School Board, was located on the northwest corner of Baltimore and Highland Avenues and is shown here shortly after it opened in 1905. The library, now under the auspices of the Borough Council, continues to effectively serve the borough.

This view of Baltimore Avenue looking east from in front of Borough Hall shows trolley tracks being laid just after the turn of the century.

48

Proud workmen from the DeSales Carriage and Wagon Works pose with their recently constructed wagon in front of their shop on the southwest corner of Baltimore and Highland Avenues, c. 1900. When the age of the automobile arrived, DeSales became a car dealership.

In this 1952 photograph, Farrello Motors, a Studebaker parts and service dealership, is preparing to close shop after thirty years of serving the borough. Barksdale Studios, a photographic studio operating nationally, relocated to this building.

Because Baltimore Avenue carried so many automobiles, it became a popular location for service stations, as can be seen in this 1928 photograph of the northwest corner of Wycombe Avenue.

Dr. H.C. Bartleson was one of the many physicians who practiced from home offices in the borough. Bartleson's home, shown here in 1897, still stands on the northeast corner of Baltimore and Wycombe Avenues, but it is difficult to recognize: it has been turned into a laundromat.

American Legion Post 65 purchased a private house at what is now Baltimore Avenue and Legion Terrace in the early 1920s. The building was remodeled to serve the members of Post 65.

This 1920s photograph shows the social side of the Legion Hall's use, but more importantly, the hall served as meeting place for advocates of veteran's rights. It was sold and demolished in the 1960s.

The Evergreen Lodge, shown here in 1906, was originally constructed as a private residence on Baltimore Avenue between Rigby Avenue and Legion Terrace. It was converted into an inn to serve Philadelphians seeking to escape the hot city during the summer months.

The Evergreen Lodge was demolished to make room for this service station and the growing business district along Baltimore Avenue, as shown in this 1927 photograph.

By the time this 1928 photograph was taken, the easy availability of automobiles began to change the nature of the community. At Baltimore Avenue and Legion Terrace, affordable houses on smaller lots allowed an increasing number of city dwellers to move in. Many Philadelphians sought to escape what was thought to be a more dirty and dangerous environment in order to achieve the "American dream."

The Lansdowne Storage Warehouse on West Baltimore Avenue, shown in 1905, was constructed by Richardson Shoemaker, a prominent resident who operated a livery business from this building. The building still stands, though entombed in brick.

Shoemaker didn't have much of a commute, as he lived next door in this house, photographed *c.* 1905. Today the site is the parking lot for the Blockbuster Video store.

Shoemaker also owned a four-story concrete building on South Lansdowne Avenue, located at the southern end of the bank building at Baltimore and Lansdowne Avenues. He sold the property to the bank, even though the bank only wanted the land, and he then had the storage building moved next to his other warehouse around the corner, as shown in this 1925 photograph. The building was demolished in 1987 to make way for a parking lot.

This 1902 photograph shows the trolley switch on Baltimore Avenue, just west of St. John's Church. The switch was necessary because it allowed one trolley to pull out of the way while another passed by on this single-track route.

This house, photographed in 1905, was located at 24 West Baltimore Avenue and was demolished as the borough's business district moved west.

This twin house was constructed on the lawn of the Mary Owen House in 1902. The Runnemede Club, owners of the Owen House at the turn of the century, developed the front lawn to provide a source of income for its own operation.

These wonderful homes at 124 and 126 West Baltimore Avenue are shown in 1906, adorned with shields of various designs, open porches, and large rooftop pediments.

Baltimore Avenue is shown looking east from Windermere Avenue during renovation work to the trolley line, c. 1903.

By the time this property on the northwest corner of Baltimore and Windermere Avenues was photographed in 1928, Lansdowne's larger properties were being subdivided, and homes were being constructed for those fleeing Philadelphia.

In 1906, a trolley travels past The Windermere, a private home converted into a inn. The Windermere sits on Baltimore Avenue at Windermere Terrace and is an apartment house today.

The Windermere was an elegant escape from the hustle and bustle of the city, as evidenced in this 1906 photograph of one of its parlors.

Gladstone Hall, considered by many to be the grandest house ever built in Lansdowne, was located in present-day Gladstone Manor. The house, photographed before 1900, was built for Charles Kelly, owner of the Kellyville Mill. Later, the property was purchased by Philip J. Walsh, an Irish immigrant and successful merchant who operated a department store on Second Street in Philadelphia. The estate was comprised of 52 acres extending as far away as West Greenwood Avenue. Mr. Walsh was killed in an accident while on vacation in 1893. His family retained ownership of the property until the late 1920s, when it was sold to W. Percival Johnson, who developed Gladstone Manor.

After the manor was developed, Gladstone Hall was used as a meeting place for the Gladstone Manor Civic Association until the structure was razed in 1935. This is the elegant parlor of Gladstone Hall, photographed prior to 1900.

Johnson left Gladstone Hall intact after developing Gladstone Manor and used the building as a meeting place for residents of the housing development. This pre-1900 photograph shows the front porch of the building.

Four

School Days

The Upper Darby School Board, which operated the schools in what is today Lansdowne (prior to the borough's incorporation in 1893), constructed Lansdowne School beginning with this building in the late 1880s on Baltimore and Highland Avenues. This photograph dates from pre-1900 and reveals the building's beautiful brickwork, roof cresting, and elaborate chimneys. Prior to the 1920s it was possible that a student could complete their schooling, kindergarten through twelfth grade, in one building. Additions were constructed as the school population increased until 1910, when the building reached its maximum square footage. Just as the building grew in stages, it was demolished in stages, beginning in 1950 and lasting until the final portion was razed for the Lansdowne Fire Company's headquarters, which was dedicated in 1986.

The lawn in front of Lansdowne School served as a gathering spot for students and was used by this physical fitness class, c. 1902.

The Class of 1918 posed for a group photograph at Lansdowne School.

In this undated photograph of the Lansdowne School staff, the much-beloved and respected Emilie Groce stands in the second row, fourth from the left. Groce served as both a teacher and principal during her long career in Lansdowne.

It may not look like fun, but I'm sure students enjoyed the small gymnasium at Lansdowne School, *c.* 1902.

FOOTBALL BANQUET
LANSDOWNE HIGH SCHOOL
SEASON 1919

JAN. 31ST 1920
KUGLER'S

For decades, Lansdowne High School has taken pride in fielding great football teams. In this 1920 photograph, the team celebrates a successful season. The guest of honor, Eddie Collins, is seated at the top center of the image. Collins, a member of the Baseball Hall of Fame, lived in Lansdowne while he played for the Philadelphia Athletics Baseball Club.

On April 23, 1963, a portion of the Lansdowne School that ran along the Highland Avenue sidewalk burned.

The young women of Lansdowne High School also had an opportunity to participate in team sports such as basketball and, as shown in this 1921 photograph, field hockey.

With the population of the borough steadily increasing, by the 1920s it was obvious that it was necessary to build a separate high school. The Green Avenue site was chosen partly because it was adjacent to Stewart Field. The high school building was considered one of the finest public school facilities in the country when it opened.

Lansdowne High School was the center of the social life of the borough's students. Organized dances such as this 1940s event were regularly held in the school's gymnasium.

The school's auditorium was the site of many assemblies which brought the entire student body together, as in this 1940s scene.

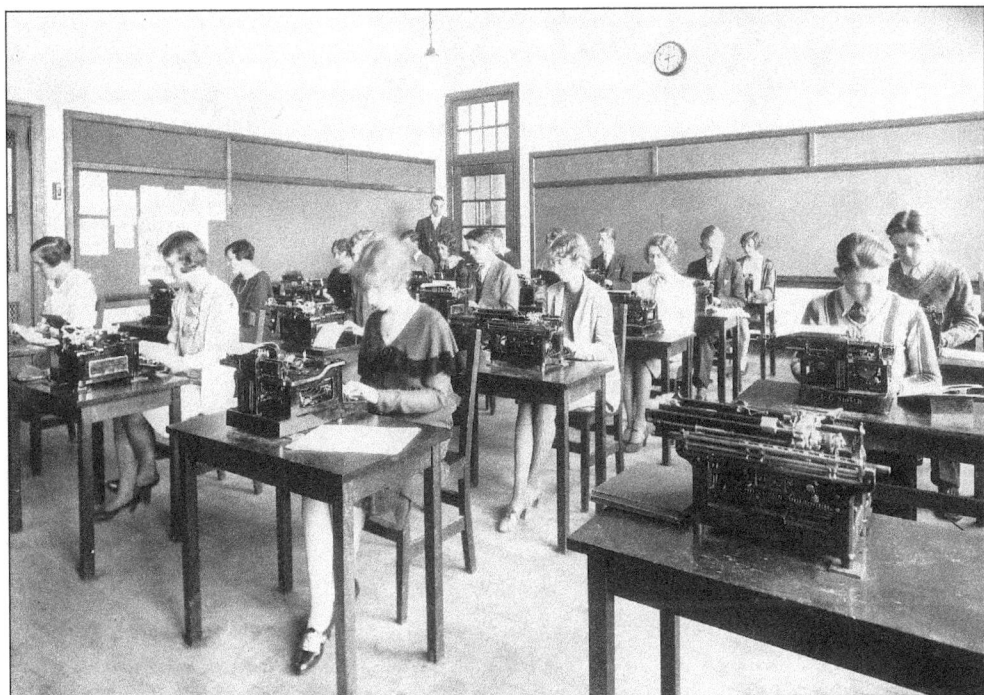

Lansdowne High School was long known for its rigorous academic curriculum, and as a result, it attracted students from throughout the county who paid tuition to attend. The school also provided a commercial program, as depicted in this photograph of a typing class, c. 1930.

The heaviest growth in the borough's population occurred in the western end. When Griffith's Lake was ordered drained and filled in the 1920s, land became available for the construction of the Ardmore Avenue Elementary School.

Stewart Field hosted Lansdowne High School sporting events from around 1900 to the early 1980s. Here, Paul Gallagher gains yardage in a 1951 game.

Taken from a helicopter, this *c.* 1960 view shows the extensive campus of Lansdowne High School. At the top of the photograph is Stewart Field (created *c.* 1902). In the center are Lansdowne High School (opened in 1929) and the Green Avenue Elementary School (built in 1949).

Five

The War Effort

World War I ushered in the reality of the outside world to Lansdowne. For the first time, Lansdowne's sons were called off to foreign lands, some never to return. During the two World Wars, residents rallied to support the soldiers by producing clothing, recycling scrap metals and paper, planting "victory gardens," and forming civil defense units. When the wars were over, sons who had made the supreme sacrifice were remembered with memorial windows in churches and through monuments erected in their honor. On Armistice Day 1921, residents and grieving families joined together to dedicate the Lansdowne School World War Monument, which sat in front of the school, located at Highland and Baltimore Avenues.

During World War I, residents young and old displayed their patriotism by planting victory gardens. These efforts were encouraged by Lansdowne School teacher Miss Emilie Groce, who later chronicled residents' war efforts in her 1919 book, *Lansdowne School and the World War*, from which this photograph is taken.

After World War I, the Clinton Wunderlich American Legion Post 65 was created to meet the needs of returning veterans. The post's namesake, Clinton Wunderlich, was the first Lansdowne resident to be killed in the war. In 1927 the post's marching band gathered in front of its headquarters at Legion Terrace. In the front row, the first drummer on the left is Joseph Doan, who is still active in all of Post 65's activities.

JUNK RALLY
For LANSDOWNE
and vicinity

Monday, 7.30 P.M.

SEPTEMBER 14, 1942

—*at*—

No.th Lansdowne
and LaCrosse Aves.

(NEXT TO A. & P. MARKET)

Junk helps make guns,
tanks, ships for our fighting men . . . .
Bring in anything made
of metal or rubber . . . .

or see your Post Warden

Bring your family
Meet your friends

Throw YOUR scrap into the fight!

JUNK MAKES FIGHTING WEAPONS

One old radiator will provide
scrap steel needed for seventeen .30 calibre rifles.

One old lawn mower will
help make six 3-inch shells.

One useless old tire
will provide as much
rubber as is used in
12 gas masks.

One old shovel will
help make 4 hand
grenades.

Let's Jolt them with Junk
from Lansdowne

Because of various shortages during World War II, "scrap" or "junk rallies" were held all around the country. In this September 1942 *Delaware County Daily News* advertisement, readers were urged to recycle materials, which were portrayed as going directly to the war effort. War bond drives to help finance the war were held, and in both World Wars, residents' subscriptions exceeded the expectations of the federal government.

Because of food shortages, Americans were urged to create victory gardens to provide their families with food. During World War II, the Lansdowne Victory Garden Committee gathered on the stage of the Twentieth Century Club to display a portion of the residents' harvest.

During half-time of the Lansdowne vs. Swarthmore High School football game on November 24, 1950, a memorial to Lansdowne High students killed during World War II was unveiled by Reverend Maurice Gortner, Lincoln Atkiss (left), executive director of the memorial committee, and Albert Beers, burgess of Lansdowne. Funding for the erection of the monument and cement bleachers was donated by Lansdowne residents.

Six

Houses of Worship

Religious institutions have long played an important role in Lansdowne, whether serving residents' spiritual needs, educating children, or serving community interests. Early in the borough's development, real estate developers were anxious to establish houses of worship to attract homeowners to the community. This photograph is labeled, "May 28, 1907, Five Evangelical Pastors of Lansdowne—The Dog (5) has made over 1,500 pastoral calls." From left to right the pastors are: Crosswell McBee (St. John's Episcopal Church), Edward Bird (Lansdowne Baptist Church), J.R.T. Gray (Lansdowne Methodist Church), and William Boyd (First Presbyterian Church). The dog belonged to Reverend Boyd, who named him Prince after his alma mater, Princeton.

The Lansdowne Friends Meeting House was the first religious building constructed in the borough, c. 1831. For several years prior to this building's construction, the Friends met in a wheelwright shop on the northwest corner of Baltimore and Lansdowne Avenues. Notice the now-demolished house to the south of the meeting house in this c. 1900 photograph.

The interior of the Lansdowne Friends Meeting House is shown here just after the turn of the century.

Jacob R. Elfreth, and Isaac P. and Sarah Garrett, members of the Friends Meeting, pose on the porch of the meeting house, c. 1900. Garrett served as postmaster of Lansdowne from 1869 to 1914, and then again from 1921 to 1923.

A small burial ground for the Society of the New Jerusalem was located north of Marshall Road near the end of Wycombe Avenue. The cemetery pictured here c. 1910 was relocated in the 1960s when a portion of the site was developed.

When the members of the First Presbyterian Church of Lansdowne gathered in this photograph on October 18, 1887, to lay the cornerstone of their church, the area which was to become Greenwood and Owen Avenues had been planted with corn.

Quickly outgrowing the 1887 sanctuary, the First Presbyterian Church of Lansdowne constructed the building on the right, laying the cornerstone in 1915. This 1930s photograph shows both buildings.

The original sanctuary was demolished in 1949 to make room for a church school addition. The foundation of the original building was left intact and used in the construction of the new building.

Reverend Boyd and his dog Prince join with church members to celebrate the 20th anniversary of the First Presbyterian Church of Lansdowne.

In 1888, St. John the Evangelist Church constructed this chapel on the southwest corner of Baltimore and Union Avenues.

With the growth of the church's membership and a desire for a more prominent location, St. John's began construction of its new church in 1900 at the corner of Lansdowne and Baltimore Avenues.

In the mid-1880s, the newly formed Baptist Church rejected the offer by early real estate developer Homer C. Stewart to build their church on East Stewart Avenue. Instead, the cornerstone of the church was laid in 1887 at the corner of Lansdowne and LaCrosse Avenues, as shown in this 1897 photograph.

On June 2, 1895, the first services were held at the Lansdowne Methodist Church, with its beautiful soaring tower at the corner of Lansdowne and Stratford Avenues. This building was replaced in 1949 with a building that had a much larger seating capacity.

St. Philomena's Roman Catholic Church was originally constructed as a one-story building, as shown in this 1910s postcard. In 1925, Thomas Fitzgerald, a Philadelphia merchant and member of the church, provided the capital to construct the upper story and tower. Ever generous, Mr. Fitzgerald left a bequest to construct Fitzgerald Mercy Hospital.

St. Philomena's has a proud history of providing parochial education to generations of Lansdowne residents. The school and original church rectory are shown here in a 1910s postcard.

Seven

Civic Groups
and Leisure Time

While Lansdowne has a special rich heritage of architectural design, its people and organizations make the community unique. There is an organization dedicated to just about any interest or cause in the borough. Many have served the community for nearly one hundred years. The Lansdowne Fire Company stands out for its longevity (it has served the borough for more than a century) and the bravery of its members. In 1914 Lansdowne hosted the annual Delaware County Firemens' Convention and Parade. This view is on South Lansdowne Avenue looking north from the railroad bridge. Lansdowne has been the home of many people who have risen to international prominence, such as Dr. Albert Barnes and Margaret Mead. Others have made their impact on the borough itself. Whatever pursuits residents followed, Lansdowne made a lasting impression on them.

81

The Lansdowne Fire Company was organized in 1894 and posed for this photograph within its first decade of service.

Until 1912, the fire company used horse-drawn equipment in their fire-fighting efforts. The Apparatus Room in Borough Hall, showing the equipment and firemens' hats, was recorded in 1906.

The fire chief's car pulls out of Borough Hall in 1907, with Chief Cornelius F. McCollough Sr. in the passenger seat.

The housing of a new piece of equipment was always a time of excitement and celebration, as evidenced in this August 21, 1937 photograph of the housing of a new pumper.

In this 1942 *Philadelphia Bulletin* photograph are, from left to right: First Assistant Chief William Plough, Newton Walls, Chief Cornelius McCollough, and Vincent Gorman. The four are shown here riding in the company's new pumper in front of Ardmore Avenue School.

Borough Hall is readied for the 1914 Delaware County Firemens' Convention and Parade. Borough Hall was the home of the fire company from 1902 until the firehouse on Highland Avenue was constructed in 1982.

Just at the turn of the century, James T. Stewart led a successful effort to create a playground at Green and Essex Avenues. On April 15, 1929, several months before the opening of the adjacent Lansdowne High School, the borough honored this longtime resident by declaring the day Burgess James Stewart Day and by naming the playing field after this much respected and beloved man. The *Philadelphia Bulletin* captured the burgess in the inset photograph while his grandson, James Stewart II, raised the flag.

Frederick Underhill, pictured here in 1900, was affectionately known as "Uncle Fred." A champion of the Lansdowne School District, he served as a member of the school board for thirty-eight years. Ever a supporter of school activities, he often donned a school sweater and joined the high school cheerleaders on the sidelines of football games.

Seymour Eaton, shown here in the 1890s, was a newspaper journalist and author, and the founder of the Booklover's Library, a sort of turn-of-the-century "book of the month" club.

Thomas Scott, shown here in the 1870s, was the president of the Pennsylvania Railroad, one of the most powerful corporations of the nineteenth century. Scott, living in The Devonshire now on Lansdowne Court, gave Richard Griffith permission to hang the name "Lansdowne" for the first time on the railroad station in the 1870s.

Edwin Tyler Darby, a professor of dentistry at the University of Pennsylvania, lived in the borough at the turn of the century. He was so admired by his students that a fraternity and award for excellence in dentistry were named in his honor.

St. John's baseball team sits for a portrait at the Lansdowne Cricket Field at the southwest corner of Baltimore and Union Avenues in 1900. The manager, James T. Stewart, is the man wearing the suit at the center of the photograph.

A baseball umpire and player from the Pembroke team (Pembroke was the previous name of East Lansdowne) pose on the baseball field on Union and McKinley Avenues, c. 1900. It was on this field that the Union Athletic Association began its activities, including fielding various teams and celebrating the Fourth of July.

A borough cricket team, *c.* 1900, poses for a turn-of-the-century photograph at the Lansdowne Cricket Field.

During the years of segregation, Delaware County had a "Negro League." Lansdowne's entry, the Lansdowne Athletic Club, played its home games on the Lansdowne Cricket Field. In the rear is the sign for the W.L. Cummings Chemical Co., an early radium processing company. This building was declared a Superfund Site by the Environmental Protection Agency and razed in the 1990s.

BRUINS
1959-60

The Lansdowne Boys Club has served thousands of boys since its founding in the 1940s. The Boys Club added an ice hockey program in 1959, which lasted only one year. The team played at the rink in the Lansdowne Ice and Coal plant in East Lansdowne. The Lansdowne Girls Club was formed in the 1970s. Both clubs are now thriving, offering baseball, softball, basketball, and soccer programs.

Neil Mershon (center of photograph), a lifelong Lansdowne resident and ardent bicycle enthusiast, joins friends Al Irwin and Betty Snyder in 1931 at Stewart Field. Several generations of the Mershon family have dazzled residents with their cycling feats in the borough's Fourth of July parades.

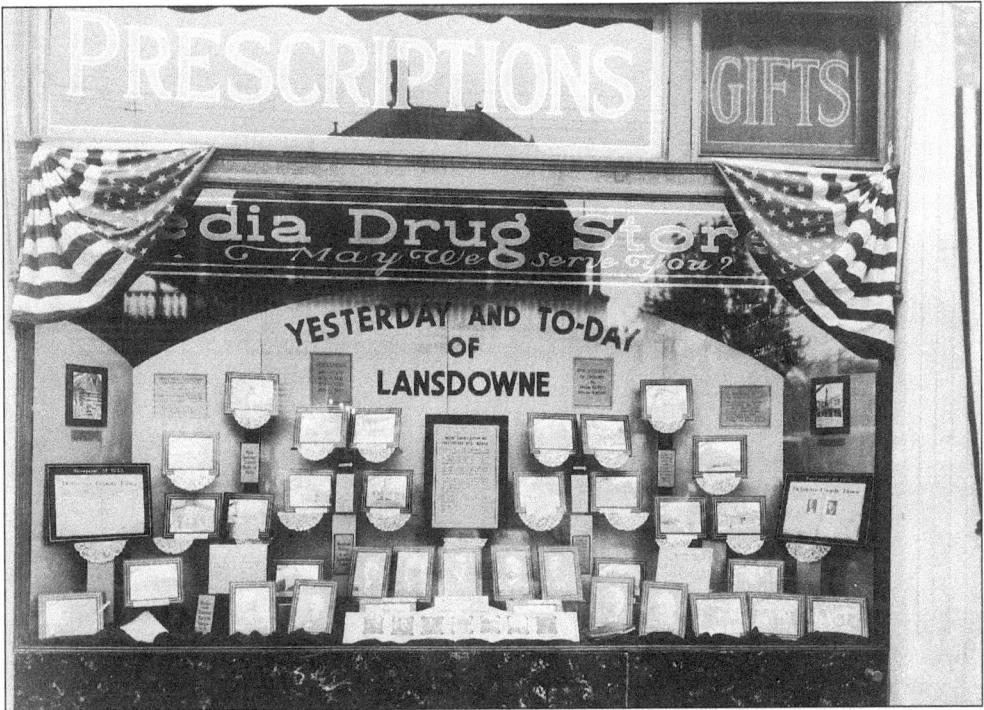

Lansdowne has long celebrated its history, as is evidenced by this 1952 window display at the Media Drugstore on the northwest corner of Lansdowne and Baltimore Avenues. Several photographs featured in this book originally appeared in this exhibit.

In this 1960s Fourth of July photograph, Mayor William Helms (in the passenger seat) rides with Neil Mershon in his coal-burning Stanley Steamer.

The Twentieth Century Club was founded as a community service organization in 1897 by Lansdowne residents concerned with issues faced by women. The Clubhouse at Lansdowne Avenue and Lansdowne Court was built in 1911.

The Clubhouse has been at the center of the Lansdowne social life for decades. Players in a 1921 Lansdowne High School theatrical production pose on its stage. The Clubhouse has been turned over to the borough and hosted many borough centennial events in 1993.

The Lansdowne Country Club was photographed in 1902, the year of its organization. Located in the Isaac Jones House, on Baily Road, it offered members golf, tennis, and field hockey, and served as a major gathering location for socializing.

The Lansdowne Country Club relocated several times, but its Baily Road site between Wycombe and South Lansdowne Avenues was the most beautiful, as shown in this 1905 photograph of the golf course as it slopes down the valley toward the borough of Darby.

Lansdowne has abounded with youth organizations over the last century. In 1911, Boy Scout Troop 1 (now Troop 63) from the First Presbyterian Church posed for a photograph. They are: (front row) Walter Ebrey, Allison, Paul Callow, Alf Warren, Arthur Dewar, and Donald McLean; (second row) ? Winchester, William Ziegler, Cook McLean, Louis McLean, Harrison Matsinger, and Leslie Nicholson; (third row) Fred Lewis, Edward Maloney, Eugene Baker, Clinton Wunderlich, and Haviland Wright; (back row) Scoutmaster Alfred Steer, Rush Fackler, Archie Dunlap, Craig Greiner, Paul Wright, and Charles Powell. On a sad note, Albert Clinton Wunderlich would be dead within the decade, serving his country in World War I. Many of the other boys also took up arms during the war.

Gardening and tree planting have always been an integral part of peoples' lives in the borough. In this 1902 photograph, a gardener tends plants in his backyard. The west side of Rigby Avenue can be seen in the rear.

The Lansdowne Symphony Orchestra gathers for its first concert in 1947. The orchestra originated at the First Presbyterian Church (where this photograph was taken) and was led by Larry Ustick (sitting in the foreground on the left with a violin). The orchestra just celebrated fifty years of making music and is considered one of the finest community orchestras in the nation.

In this 1923 photograph, high school student Robert Deans assists Officer Frank Emery in directing traffic at the corner of Lansdowne and Baltimore Avenues.

Amy Albertson (left) plays dolls with a friend along Highland Avenue just north of Greenwood Avenue in the 1890s.

Eight

Neighborhoods and Homes

Lansdowne is a community comprised of many distinct neighborhoods, each uniquely reflecting the era in which it developed. The small neighborhoods of eighteenth-century workers' and managers' houses are a reflection of early industries along the Darby Creek. The large nineteenth-century houses on Lansdowne Avenue represent the emergence and growth of the middle class. Gladstone Manor is a 1920s orderly neighborhood built to look like an English village, while a grouping of 1930s Spanish Revival houses on Wabash Avenue represents a more exotic view of the world. Our newer neighborhoods, like Coral Hills with its split-level homes, signify the modern age with their prominent garages representing America's love of the car. A middle-class family is shown here posing on their open porch at 28 Dudley Avenue, c. 1900.

The Walton children pose *c.* 1900 for their father, George Walton, on the front lawn of The Shadelands, which was located on Shadeland Avenue at about where Berkeley Avenue is today. The children are, from left to right: Peg, Grace, Anne, Virginia, Linda, and Kirby.

This *c.* 1900 winter photograph shows the view from the upper story of the Waltons' home on Shadeland Avenue. The Waltons operated a small farm on this property which produced food for their own table and enough milk to establish a small dairy business.

Kirby Walton, standing at the gate on the right side of the photograph, inspects his family's cows. The structure behind him was the family's ice house, c. 1900.

The Shadelands property began on Shadeland Avenue, ran along the back of the properties along the north side of the houses on Berkeley Avenue to east of Eldon Avenue, and then along the rear property line of the houses on Essex Avenue. Peg Walton, daughter of George Walton, feeds the family's chickens.

Peg, Grace, and Anne Walton are standing at what is today the intersection of Eldon and Berkeley Avenues, *c.* 1900. The small creek ran along Eldon Avenue and served as a source of ice for the farm's ice house.

Grace Walton poses at the rear of the Scott Estate, *c.* 1900. Within a decade this property would be developed as Lansdowne Court.

The same view in 1918, after Lansdowne Court was developed. By then the Frank Furness-designed Devonshire had been converted into apartments to accommodate the growing number of people who wanted to live in the popular borough.

Griffith's Park, created in 1912, has long fascinated Lansdowne residents. The lake was fed by a stream running from another small lake on Marshall Road. Horace Griffith, a local real estate developer, constructed the lake by simply damming the stream as it ran over the area comprising what is today the ballfield at Ardmore Avenue School. He used the lake to attract buyers to the building lots he owned in the neighborhoods that surrounded the attraction. By the mid-1910s Griffith suffered financial problems and ceased to maintain the park.

In 1921, Duane Elliot, a four year old from the neighborhood, drowned in the lake, forcing Griffith to drain what had become a swamp-like area. Trees planted along the edge of the property and a small stone wall on the lower playground remain today as a reminder of Griffith's Park.

Another natural wonder of Lansdowne is its 350-year-old sycamore tree living at 47 East LaCrosse Avenue. Shown in 1900, this tree will soon become the centerpiece of a public park celebrating this beautiful and awe-inspiring legacy to each of us.

S.P. Levis climbed to the roof of the Shoemaker Stable in 1900 to capture this view of Lansdowne Park, now an historic district listed on the National Register of Historic Places. In the center of the photograph is St. John the Evangelist Church, with the tower of the Lansdowne Methodist Church prominently showing at the right along the tops of the trees. Lansdowne Park was developed beginning in 1889 by Homer C. Stewart and Edward Price and features numerous styles of Victorian architecture. The Neighbor's Club, still active today, was formed by residents

of this development to provide town watch services prior to the creation of the borough. Evident are the twin towers on the houses at the corners of Owen and LaCrosse Avenues and the single tower at LaCrosse and Runnemede Avenues. An historic district marker telling the history of Lansdowne Park is permanently installed on the lawn of First Union Bank at Runnemede and Baltimore Avenues.

Amy Albertson (on the left) and a friend ride along Runnemede Avenue, c. 1900. The house on the southeast corner of Runnemede and LaCrosse Avenues had yet to be built.

Lansdowne's oldest house that is still standing is the Mary Owen House at 12 Owen Avenue. Built in 1732, this building has served as both a residence and a mens' club.

Charles Pilling, a Philadelphia-based surgical instrument manufacturer, extensively remodeled this house at 42 Windermere Avenue and constructed what was certainly the most extensive garden the borough has ever seen.

Designed in a Japanese style, the garden featured a fish pond, shown here in 1906, and several small bridges, greenhouses, and many varieties of imported plants native to Japan. The gardens were periodically open to the public and proved to be quite popular.

Lansdowne Park featured various style of "modern" homes including this Colonial Revival house at 20 Owen Avenue, c. 1905.

While most of Lansdowne Park was constructed by real estate developers, there were exceptions. This 1904 photograph shows 55 Owen Avenue, which the Crowley family had built for themselves.

No. 30 Runnemede Avenue, shown here in 1906, is a beautiful example of Romanesque Revival design. This style is easily identified by the use of stone and the oversized rounded tower protruding from the roof.

Lansdowne Park children play on the side lawn of 73 West LaCrosse Avenue. Runnemede Avenue is in the background of this *c.* 1900 photograph.

No. 59 and 61 Owen Avenue are examples of houses constructed by developers in Lansdowne Park. East Stratford Avenue, the first block off of Lansdowne Avenue prior to the construction of any houses, can be seen in the background of this *c.* 1900 photograph.

By 1912, Lansdowne Park had been fully developed. No. 35 and 37 Windermere Avenue are examples of later homes constructed within the original boundaries of the development.

110

Margaret Mary and Jay McLaughlin stand on the lawn of their home at 35 West LaCrosse in 1942. Lansdowne Park remains popular because of its centralized location and pedestrian-friendly design. No. 55 Owen Avenue is in the background.

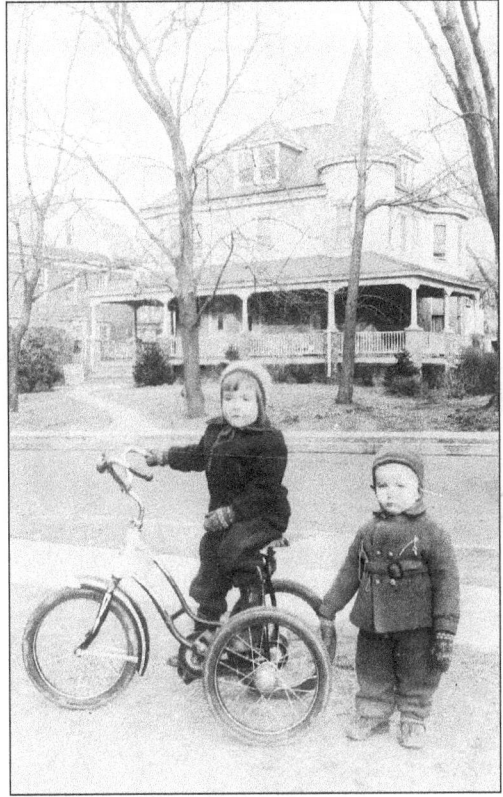

Homes on the southeast corner of Stewart and Owen Avenues were constructed just after the turn of the century by prolific Lansdowne builder William Shuster. Shuster built a reputation as a very skilled contractor, and his houses were dubbed "Shuster-built." The Methodist church tower is prominently shown in the background.

In the late 1880s, Henry Albertson, a dry goods merchant, purchased a large lot which today includes Balfour Circle, portions of Lansdowne, East Greenwood, Wycombe, and Stewart Avenues, and all of Price and Clover Avenues. Albertson had this house, 135 North Lansdowne Avenue (now Balfour Circle), built in the 1880s. He then subdivided the remainder of his land, and went on to build numerous houses, which he either rented out or sold. Balfour Circle, developed in the 1920s, now covers the site of the garden in this 1890s photograph. This neighborhood maintains much of its turn-of-the-century appearance and is currently being considered for inclusion in the National Register of Historic Places.

In 1906, local real estate salesman C. Edwin Hunter offered these houses on the north side of East Greenwood Avenue for sale, just east of Lansdowne Avenue. Hunter operated an office in Philadelphia and used photographs such as this one to entice city residents to consider moving to the borough.

No. 23 East Greenwood Avenue has long been known as "the Castle" because of its prominent tower and because the original owner, Marie Brolasky, was reputed to be a European countess. Shown in 1919, Eugene, Harry, Melville, and Marshall Case pose on the porch of the Castle.

This 1905 photograph, looking east from in front of 23 East Greenwood Avenue, reveals the early appearance of the street prior to its paving and construction. At this time East Greenwood was the northern-most developed neighborhood in the borough. Farmland and the newly created Lansdowne Playground (later to be called Stewart Field) sat behind the north side of the street.

Frederick Taylor Pusey stands on the porch of his home at 33 East Greenwood Avenue in 1903. Pusey, an attorney, served as a state representative and borough solicitor. This was later the home of Jacob Verlenden, a prominent resident whose family operated mills in Darby for several generations.

No. 38 and 44 East Greenwood Avenue stand prominently on the south side of the avenue in 1906. While Henry Albertson built numerous houses in the neighborhood, the majority of the land was sold as undeveloped lots and purchasers commissioned architects to design customized houses such as these buildings.

By the time this photograph of 51 East Greenwood Avenue was taken in 1907, most of the street had been developed, with only four lots remaining from the thirty-two lots Henry Albertson laid out in the 1880s.

In 1896, James Perkins purchased six lots from Henry Albertson and constructed the twin houses at 83–85, 99–101, and 91–93 (shown here) East Greenwood Avenue in 1906. Perkins sold off five of the houses and used his profit to pay the construction costs of his own house at 99 East Greenwood Avenue. This was a very common practice throughout the borough.

T. Houard Wright, an executive with the Insurance Company of North America, designed his own home at 107 East Greenwood Avenue in the 1890s and posed with his family in 1900 on its front lawn. The family members are, from left to right: Paul, Edith (in the chair with William), Franklin (standing), Haviland (sitting), Houard, Emily, and Thomas (kneeling).

No. 130 North Wycombe sits frozen in time on the Fourth of July 1900. Wycombe Avenue was previously named Kenney's Lane after a farm located further south along the windy road. This is the eastern-most edge of the Albertson property.

This photograph of Wycombe Avenue, north of Greenwood Avenue, was taken in 1902, when the road was little more than a cow path. It wasn't until the automobile and the construction of the Marshall Road Bridge in Upper Darby over Cobbs Creek leading into Philadelphia that this street attracted traffic. Previously, most people entered the borough from the east either on Baltimore Avenue or via the railroad.

At the turn of the century, Lansdowne had no fewer than three sizable floral greenhouses within its boundaries. William Leonard, the Pennock family, and August Valentine Doemling produced a steady stream of flowers to be sent into Philadelphia and New York City. The concentration of greenhouses in the borough spurred the creation of several hauling companies. Robert Robinson Jr. began what became Robinson Moving and Storage by hauling flowers to market. This photograph, taken from the west side of North Wycombe Avenue just north of Greenwood Avenue, shows the Rose Farm greenhouses on Union Avenue owned by August V. Doemling. Doemling also owned the clay tennis courts in the foreground. His daughter, Betty Doemling, operated the Rose Farm into the 1980s when the business was sold.

C.W.R. Smith and his wife relax on the porch of their home at 59 Price Avenue in 1911. Prior to the development of houses, Price Avenue housed extensive greenhouses.

This house on the northwest corner of Stewart and Highland Avenues is rumored to have been built for the 1876 Centennial Celebration held in Philadelphia's Fairmount Park. It is quite possibly true, as only a few of the celebration's buildings were constructed to be permanent. This building, as shown in 1908, would have been considered among the temporary structures which were either moved to other sites or razed.

These six houses, constructed and sold by Locke and Cronin, are on the south side of East Stewart Avenue beginning at the southwest corner at Wycombe Avenue. When this 1907 photograph was taken, the American Four Square design (the style of these buildings) was the most popular in the borough.

A hitching post stands ready for a horse in front of 29 East Stratford Avenue (the northwest corner of Stratford and Highland Avenues), c. 1902.

Mrs. Stephen Levis proudly poses for her husband on the front porch of their new home at 24 North Maple Avenue in 1905.

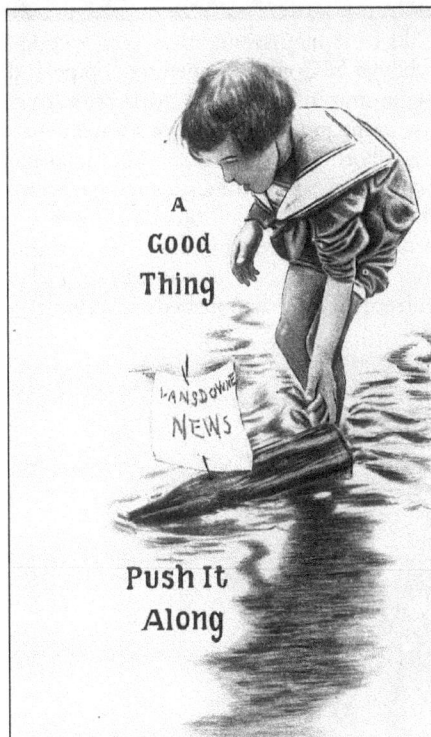

A Good Thing

LANSDOWNE NEWS

Push It Along

Over the years, Lansdowne has been the home of several newspapers including *The Lansdowne News*, begun in 1897, which became *The Lansdowne Times* in 1911. Many of the photographs in this book were taken by S.P. Levis, owner of *The Lansdowne News*. This advertisement for the publication appeared c. 1900.

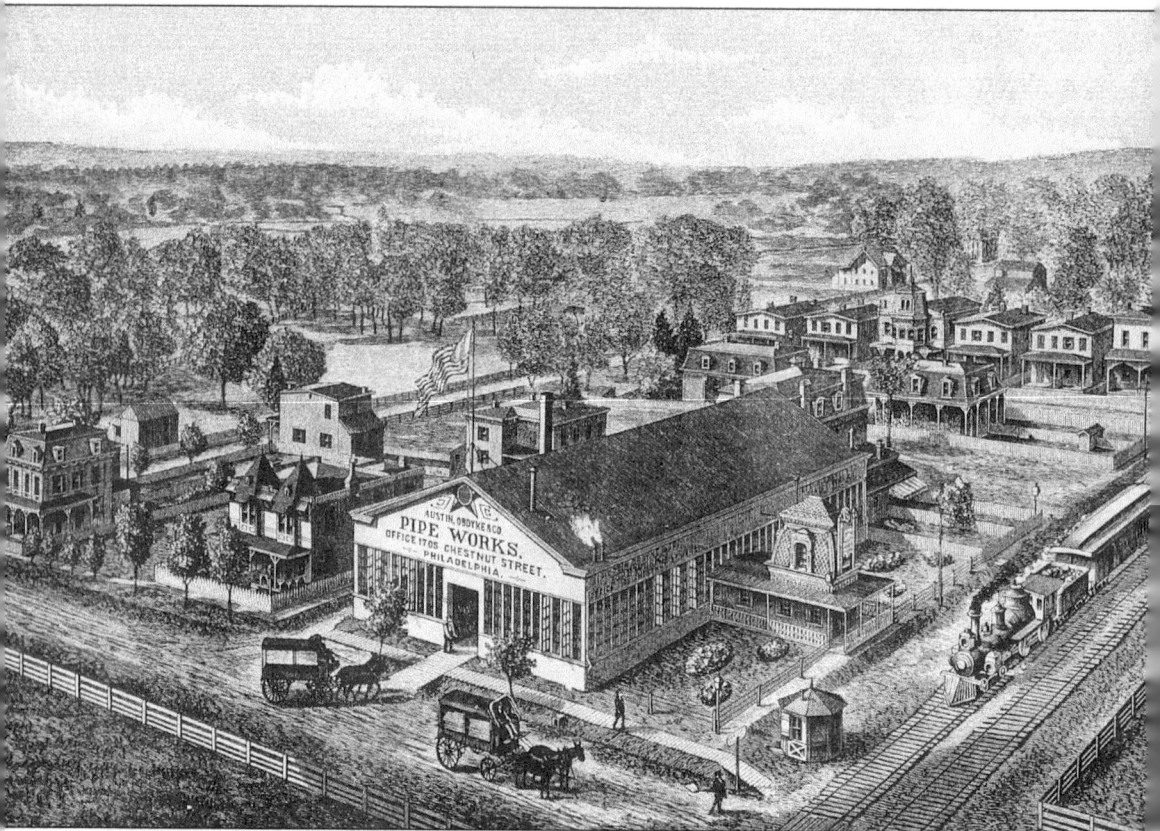

Odd as it may seem, there was a company town within what today is Lansdowne. Austin, Obdyke & Company operated a pipe and pressed tin plant on Union Avenue and the railroad beginning in the 1880s. In addition to constructing the plant shown in this 1884 lithograph, the company built numerous tenements on Austin, Union, Nyack, and Maple Avenues. This neighborhood assumed the unofficial name of "Tintown" because of the tenements' tin roofs and the pressed-tin facades on some of the structures. The plant building was demolished by the Environmental Protection Agency after it was discovered that it was used as a radium processing plant during the 1910s. Contaminated byproducts from the plant were used as mortar in a number of buildings in eastern Delaware County. Buildings containing these materials are currently being demolished and rebuilt.

In the early 1900s, No. 99–113 Nyack Avenue were constructed for the growing number of industrial workers at the eastern edge of the borough. Within a decade, a munitions and steel plant, a knitting mill, and a brickyard would open along South Union Avenue, joining several lumber yards and an existing milk processing plant on Baltimore Avenue and forming a diversified industrial district.

This Second Empire-style building at 56 Nyack Avenue, shown here in 1904 on the southeast corner of Nyack and Wycombe Avenues, was converted from a single family residence to an apartment house to accommodate the growing work force that powered the neighborhood's industrial businesses.

Many of the names of streets in the borough are derived from locations in England. Wycombe (as in Wycombe Avenue) is borrowed from the town of Wycombe. No. 82 South Wycombe is shown here in 1904.

The newly constructed Lansdowne Railroad Station spurred residential development in its vicinity. The house at 38–40 Nyack Avenue (shown here in 1904) was likely built to be purchased by someone who commuted to the city on a daily basis.

This beautiful house at 21 Linden Avenue reflected the middle-class ideal when the building was photographed in 1904—a single family house surrounded by trees and gardens on a quiet suburban street. It was pretty much an example of what Lansdowne offered, which was why the borough grew so quickly between 1900 and the 1940s.

To create an atmosphere of luxury and beauty, many homeowners spent as much time decorating the exterior of their homes as the interiors. The owners of 127 South Wycombe Avenue spent a great deal of energy caring for these specimen trees in 1904.

A Lansdowne police officer takes a minute to talk to a youngster in front of the Lansdowne and Darby Saving and Trust Company at Lansdowne Avenue and the railroad bridge, c. 1900.

Dick Longaker sends his brother Downs out on his *Liberty Magazine* delivery route from their home at 44 North Maple Avenue in 1926. The small town atmosphere and physical layout of Lansdowne allowed children to become fully integrated in community activities and the town's social circle.

I hope you have enjoyed reading this book and that you will hesitate before you discard those old newspapers, high school yearbooks, photographs, programs, sports uniforms, and other Lansdowne memorabilia. Many wonderful neighborhoods are not pictured in this volume, not because they are unimportant, but because they are undiscovered treasures. When you get that urge to clean the attic you can contact the author by mail at his home at: 91 East Greenwood Avenue, Lansdowne. He is always anxious to discuss Lansdowne and to receive Lansdowne memorabilia. Who knows, your photographs might be the catalyst for another book!

Acknowledgments

This book was made possible by the following, who either lent photographs, shared memories, provided technical assistance, or encouraged me to compile this book: Frances and Edward Schultz; Richard Kunkle; Debbie Sax; Dorothy Rice; Rod and Carol Walton; Paul Gallagher; Betty and Neil Mershon; Ed Biggins; Matthew and Frances O'Donnell; Donald Verlenden; Helen and Melville Case; Mimi Martin; Downs Longaker; Betty and Bob Brumbaugh; Jerry and Fran Jerome; Thomas Devon; Polly Conard Test; Barbara and Donald Kidder; George Phillips; Barbara Burt Wareham; Janet Hoopes; Dorothy Lefevre Altmaier; Marion Dunlap Mendenhall; Cindy McGoarty; John Corr; Ron Webb; Ruth Nelson, Linda Kennedy, and the Lansdowne Public Library; Thomas Smith and the Sellers Memorial Library; Robert Robinson III; Elaine Titus Latch; Elise and Connie DeLaCova; Marshall Miller and the Lansdowne Fire Company; John and Elizabeth Brumbaugh; John Nacey; Mary Albertson Thom; Doris Fredericks; William S. Wright; Joseph Heath; Frank Leas and the Borough of Media Archives; Michael Sheils, William Johnston, Joseph Doan, and American Legion Post 65; George V. Robertson Jr.; Liz and Morris Cope; George Brightbill and the Urban Archives at Temple University; Robert Barksdale; Phil Klaus Jr.; Nate Cope; Carol Baxter Eicker; David C. Titus; and Ed Hemschoot.

Finally, five special notes of thanks:

To Florence Vella who has generously given me hundreds of Stephen Levis' glass negatives. Without her gift, this book would never have been possible.

To the members and board of directors of the Greater Lansdowne Civic Association which provided the funds to print Mr. Levis' negatives.

To Gloria Pfeiffer and Judie Schultz for their review of the transcript.

To Georgeanna Juliano and Frances Schultz for assisting with photograph selection.

To Ruth Davis Hopkins Flannery for generously giving me Edwin Flannery's collection of Lansdowne memorabilia.

www.ingramcontent.com/pod-product-compliance
Lightning Source LLC
Chambersburg PA
CBHW080910100426
42812CB00007B/2233